DIY MONSTERS & MISCHIEF MAKERSPACE

MAKE A SPACE ALIEN

YOUR WAY!

RACHAEL L. THOMAS

CONSULTING EDITOR,
DIANE CRAIG,
M.A./READING SPECIALIST

abdobooks.com

Printed in the United States of America, North Mankato, Minnesota
052020
092020

THIS BOOK CONTAINS RECYCLED MATERIALS

Design: Emily O'Malley, Mighty Media, Inc.
Production: Mighty Media, Inc.
Editor: Megan Borgert-Spaniol
Cover Photographs: Mighty Media, Inc.; Shutterstock Images
Interior Photographs: iStockphoto; Mighty Media, Inc.; NASA; NASA Ames Research Center; Shutterstock Images; Tim Evanson/Flickr

The following manufacturers/names appearing in this book are trademarks:
Adhesive Tech™, Halex®, Stanley® Bostitch®

Library of Congress Control Number: 2019957667

Publisher's Cataloging-in-Publication Data
Names: Thomas, Rachael L., author.
Title: Make a space alien your way! / by Rachael L. Thomas
Description: Minneapolis, Minnesota : Abdo Publishing, 2021 | Series: DIY monsters & mischief makerspace | Includes online resources and index.
Identifiers: ISBN 9781532193217 (lib. bdg.) | ISBN 9781098211851 (ebook)
Subjects: LCSH: Handicraft for children--Juvenile literature. | Aliens--Juvenile literature. | Textile crafts--Juvenile literature. | Unidentified flying objects--Juvenile literature. | Paper work--Juvenile literature. | Refuse as art material--Juvenile literature..
Classification: DDC 745.5--dc23

Super SandCastle™ books are created by a team of professional educators, reading specialists, and content developers around five essential components—phonemic awareness, phonics, vocabulary, text comprehension, and fluency—to assist young readers as they develop reading skills and strategies and increase their general knowledge. All books are written, reviewed, and leveled for guided reading and early reading intervention programs for use in shared, guided, and independent reading and writing activities to support a balanced approach to literacy instruction.

TO ADULT HELPERS

The projects in this book are fun and simple. There are just a few things to remember to keep kids safe. Some projects may use sharp or hot objects. Also, kids may be using messy supplies. Make sure they protect their clothes and work surfaces. Be ready to offer guidance during brainstorming and assist when necessary.

CONTENTS

BECOME A MAKER

A makerspace is like a laboratory. It's a place where ideas are formed and problems are solved. Kids like you create wonderful things in makerspaces. Many makerspaces are in schools and libraries. But they can also be in kitchens, bedrooms, and backyards. Anywhere can be a makerspace when you use imagination, inspiration, **collaboration**, and problem-solving!

IMAGINATION

This takes you to new places and lets you experience new things. Anything is possible with imagination!

INSPIRATION

This is the spark that gives you an idea. Inspiration can come from almost anywhere!

Makerspace Toolbox

COLLABORATION

Makers work together. They ask questions and get ideas from everyone around them. **Collaboration** solves problems that seem impossible.

PROBLEM-SOLVING

Things often don't go as planned when you're creating. But that's part of the fun! Find creative **solutions** to any problem that comes up. These will make your project even better.

MAKE SOME MISCHIEF!

When was the last time you made mischief? Mischief is playful behavior that's goofy or surprising. Mischief can take the form of a funny **prank** or teasing trick. You can also make mischief with a team of spooky space aliens!

PROBLEM-SOLVE!
See page 26

OUT OF THIS WORLD

A space alien is a creature from outer space. Aliens play a big role in science **fiction**. But many scientists believe there may be creatures living beyond Earth. Maybe they live on moons or planets that have yet to be discovered!

IMAGINE A SPACE ALIEN

You've probably seen space aliens on TV and in movies. These aliens come from real or **fictional** planets. The most common alien image is of a skinny green body with a big head and eyes. But in a makerspace, you can make whatever crazy space alien your imagination can dream up!

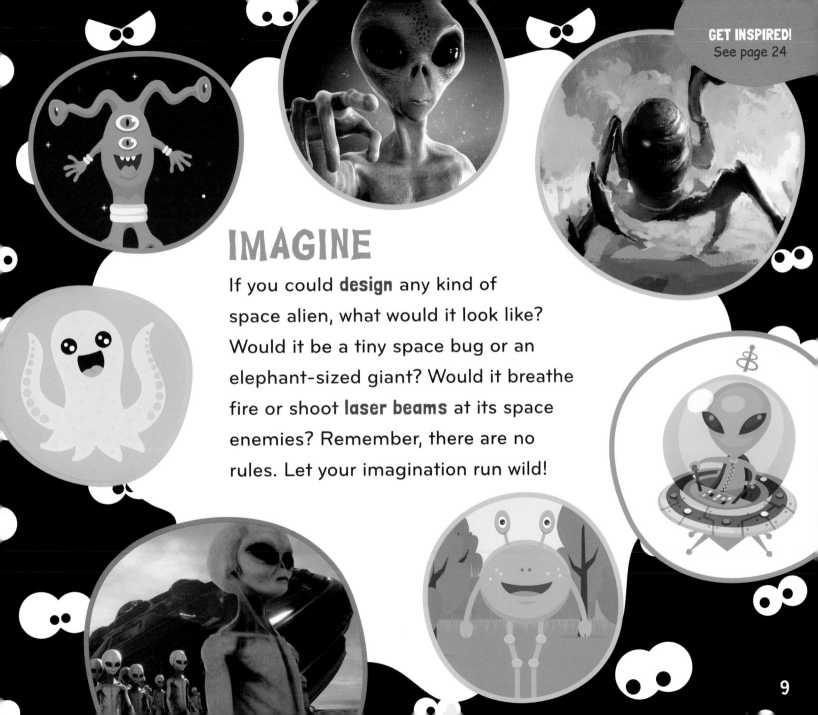

GET INSPIRED!
See page 24

IMAGINE

If you could **design** any kind of space alien, what would it look like? Would it be a tiny space bug or an elephant-sized giant? Would it breathe fire or shoot **laser beams** at its space enemies? Remember, there are no rules. Let your imagination run wild!

DESIGN A SPACE ALIEN

It's time to turn your idea into a makerspace marvel! Think about the size and shape of the space alien you imagined. Does it have a beard like a buffalo? Does it have wings like an owl? How could you use the materials around you to create these features? Where would you begin?

INSPIRATION

If you believe in aliens, go for a drive on Nevada's **Extraterrestrial** Highway! This 98-mile (158 km) stretch is famous for its many **UFO** sightings. The highway also passes by military base Area 51. Some believe the US government hides aliens at this base!

BE SAFE, BE RESPECTFUL
MAKERSPACE ETIQUETTE

COLLABORATE!
See page 28

THERE ARE JUST A FEW RULES TO FOLLOW WHEN YOU ARE CREATING YOUR SPACE ALIEN:

1. **ASK FOR PERMISSION AND ASK FOR HELP.** Make sure an adult says it's OK to make your alien. Get help when using sharp tools, such as a craft knife, or hot tools, like a glue gun.

2. **THINK IT THROUGH.** Don't give up when things don't work out exactly right. Instead, think about the problem you are having. What are some ways to solve it?

3. **SHARE THE SPACE.** Share supplies and space with other makers. Put materials away when you are finished working. Find a safe space to store unfinished projects until next time.

4. **BE NICE.** Keep your tricks and **pranks** fun or funny, but not mean. Don't make your space alien too scary for your audience. Mischief should be fun for everyone!

WHERE IS YOUR SPACE ALIEN FROM?

Which planet does your space alien call home? Knowing this will help you figure out which materials to use.

Is it from the icy ocean of Saturn's moon Enceladus?

Then it will need webbed feet and a **waterproof** body.

PROBLEM-SOLVE!
See page 26

IMAGINE

WHAT IF YOUR SPACE ALIEN LIVED ON A STAR? HOW MIGHT THIS CHANGE ITS FEATURES?

Does it live on sweltering-hot Venus?
Then give it light, airy limbs to stay cool!

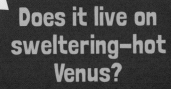

13

Dr. Penny Boston leads **NASA's** Astrobiology Institute. Astrobiology is the study of life in the universe. Dr. Boston helps NASA in its search for alien life. She also imagines what space aliens might look like and how they might behave!

Is it from Neptune, a world of freezing winds? Then it will need wings to ride the icy currents.

COLLABORATE!
See page 28

Does it live on Mars, a land of dust and rocks? Then give it hooves and goggles!

⚠ STUCK?

YOU CAN ALWAYS CHANGE YOUR MIND IN A MAKERSPACE. MAYBE YOUR ALIEN ISN'T LOOKING FIERCE ENOUGH. ADD A SECOND HEAD TO YOUR ALIEN TO ACT AS THE PREDATOR HALF!

CRAFT YOUR ALIEN

Any space alien you build will need a body. It will probably also have arms, legs, or even **tentacles**! How could you use the materials around you to build these features?

SEARCH YOUR SPACE

The perfect material might be in a coat closet, junk drawer, or even your refrigerator. Search for materials that might seem surprising!

GET INSPIRED!
See page 24

FOOTBALL

WOODEN DOWEL
AND SLINKY

BIZARRE BODY

POOL NOODLE AND FAKE FUR

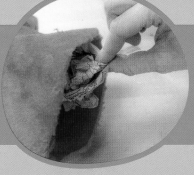

CHRISTMAS STOCKING
AND NEWSPAPER

DREADFUL HEAD

FILM CANISTERS AND
FOAM TUBES

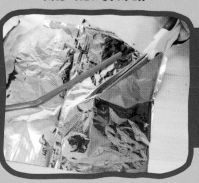

STRAWS AND CELLOPHANE

LIMBS & WINGS

17

CONNECT YOUR ALIEN

Will you keep your space alien for a long time? Or will you take it apart after you are done making mischief with it? Knowing this will help you decide what materials to use.

TOTALLY **TEMPORARY**

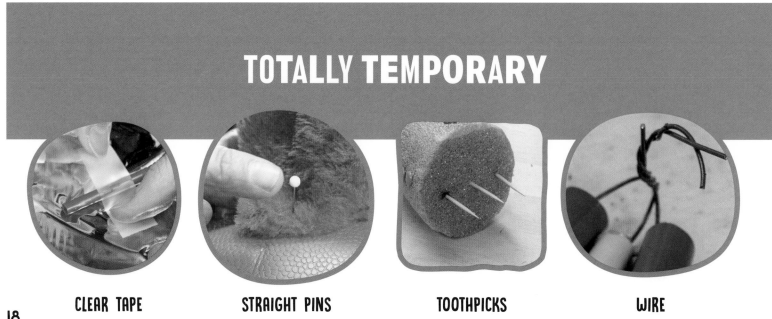

CLEAR TAPE   STRAIGHT PINS   TOOTHPICKS   WIRE

COLLABORATE!
See page 28

IMAGINE

WHAT IF YOUR ALIEN WERE FROM A PLANET WHERE IT RAINED EVERY DAY? WHAT FEATURES WOULD A CREATURE NEED TO SURVIVE IN SUCH A WET CLIMATE?

A LITTLE STICKY

GLUE DOTS

STAPLES

SUPER STICKY

DUCT TAPE

HOT GLUE

19

DECORATE YOUR ALIEN

Decorating is the final step in making your space alien. It's where you add **details** to shock and confuse others. How do these decorations help bring your strange alien to life?

EXCELLENT EYES

GOOGLY EYES AND
METAL WASHERS

METAL SPRINGS

IMAGINE

WHAT IF YOUR ALIEN CAME TO EARTH FOR VACATION? WHAT SPECIAL CLOTHING OR EQUIPMENT WOULD IT NEED TO SURVIVE ON OUR PLANET?

GET INSPIRED!
See page 24

EARS & ANTLERS

FLIPPERS & FEATHERS

YO-YOS

CHENILLE STEMS

FELT AND MARKERS

CRAFT FOAM AND POKER CHIPS

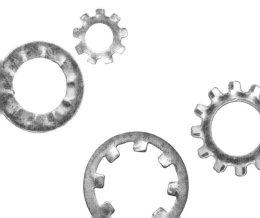

21

HELPFUL HACKS

As you work, you might discover ways to make challenging tasks easier. Try these simple tricks and **techniques** as you craft your space alien!

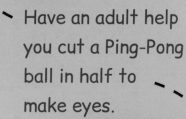

Have an adult help you cut a Ping-Pong ball in half to make eyes.

To make a stuffed body, staple together the edges of two layers of material. Leave a hole so you can reach your hand in and turn the pouch inside out. Then fill the pouch with stuffing.

PROBLEM-SOLVE!
See page 26

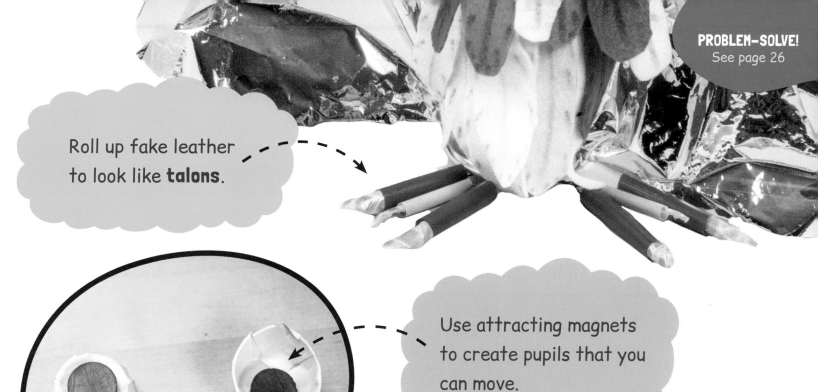

Roll up fake leather to look like **talons**.

Use attracting magnets to create pupils that you can move.

⚠ STUCK?

MAKERS AROUND THE WORLD SHARE THEIR PROJECTS ON THE INTERNET AND IN BOOKS. IF YOU HAVE A MAKERSPACE PROBLEM, THERE'S A GOOD CHANCE SOMEONE ELSE HAS ALREADY FOUND A SOLUTION. SEARCH THE INTERNET OR LIBRARY FOR HELPFUL ADVICE AS YOU MAKE YOUR PROJECTS!

GET INSPIRED

Get inspiration from the real world before you start creating your space alien!

LOOK AT NATURE

Many animals on Earth are perfectly adapted to their climates. Scales allow reptiles to live in hot, dry places. Wolves have thick fur to stay warm in the cold North. Think about the climate your alien lives in. Which animal adaptations might it find useful?

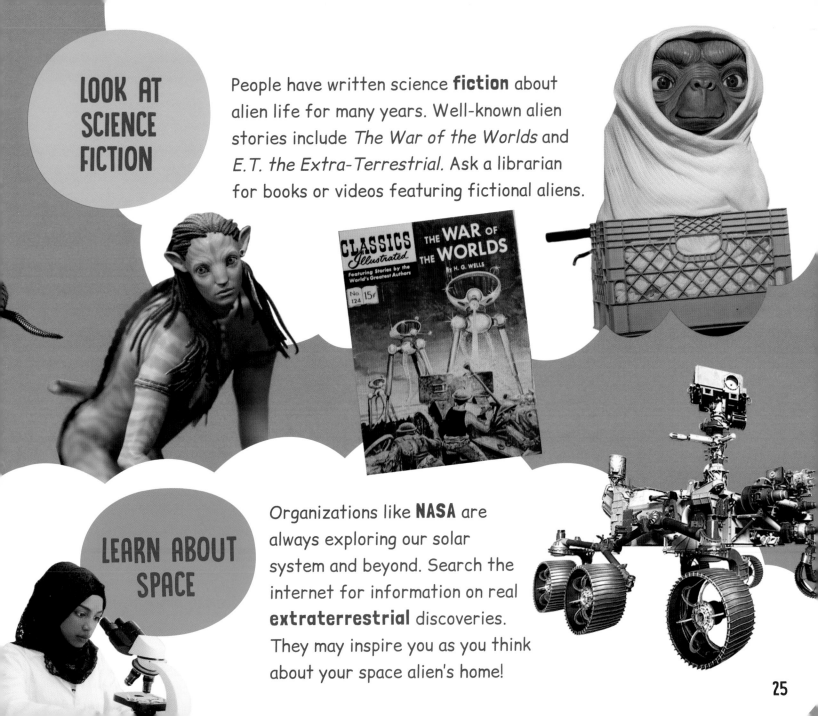

LOOK AT SCIENCE FICTION

People have written science **fiction** about alien life for many years. Well-known alien stories include *The War of the Worlds* and *E.T. the Extra-Terrestrial*. Ask a librarian for books or videos featuring fictional aliens.

CLASSICS Illustrated
Featuring Stories by the World's Greatest Authors
No. 124 15¢
THE WAR OF THE WORLDS
BY H. G. WELLS

LEARN ABOUT SPACE

Organizations like **NASA** are always exploring our solar system and beyond. Search the internet for information on real **extraterrestrial** discoveries. They may inspire you as you think about your space alien's home!

PROBLEM-SOLVE

No makerspace project goes exactly as planned. But with a little creativity, you can find a **solution** to any problem.

FIGURE OUT THE PROBLEM

Maybe your Mars space alien's horns keep falling off. Why do you think this is happening? Thinking about what is causing the problem can lead you to a solution!

SOLUTION:
INSTEAD OF USING GLUE, TIE THE HORNS FIRMLY IN PLACE WITH A CHENILLE-STEM HEADBAND.

BRAINSTORM AND TEST

Try coming up with three possible **solutions** to any problem.

Maybe the yo-yo ears aren't sticking to your alien's head. You could:

1. Make the ears out of lighter objects, such as paper cups or balloons.

2. Use a stronger connector, like hot glue, to attach the ears to the head.

3. Use the strings of the yo-yos as your connectors.

COLLABORATE

Collaboration means working together with others. There are tons of ways to collaborate to create a space alien!

ASK A FELLOW MAKER

Don't be shy about asking a friend or classmate for help on your project. Other makers can help you think through the different steps to creating your space alien. These helpers can also lend a hand during construction!

ASK AN ADULT HELPER

This could be a parent, teacher, grandparent, or any trusted adult. Tell this person about your dream alien. Your grown-up helper might think of materials or **techniques** you never would have thought of!

ASK AN EXPERT

Ask your science teacher how different plants and animals survive in Earth's many climates. Your teacher might think of features that would help your space alien survive on its planet!

THE WORLD IS A MAKERSPACE!

Your space alien may seem complete, but don't close your makerspace toolbox yet. Think about what would make your alien even more awesome. What would you do differently if you made it again? What would happen if you used different **techniques** or materials?

IMAGINATION

INSPIRATION

COLLABORATION

PROBLEM-SOLVING

DON'T STOP AT SPACE ALIENS

You can use your makerspace toolbox beyond the makerspace! You might use it to accomplish everyday tasks, such as **designing** the perfect tree house or knitting a scarf. But makers use the same toolbox to do big things. One day, these tools could help launch a fashion trend or invent a new video game. Turn your world into a makerspace! What problems could you solve?

GLOSSARY

collaborate – to work with others.

design – to plan how something will appear or work.

detail – a small part of something.

equipment – a set of tools or items used for a special purpose or activity.

extraterrestrial – a creature from outer space or another planet.

fiction – stories that are not real.

laser beam – a very narrow, intense beam of light that can be used for cutting things.

NASA – National Aeronautics and Space Administration. NASA is a US government agency that manages the nation's space program and conducts flight research.

prank – a trick done to someone as a joke.

solution – an answer to, or a way to solve, a problem.

talon – the claw of an animal, especially that of a bird of prey.

technique – a method or style in which something is done.

tentacle – a long, flexible limb on an invertebrate such as a jellyfish or squid.

UFO – an unidentified flying object.

waterproof – made so that water can't get in.